COMMENDATIONS

I am delighted to commend this powerful little book. Christopher brings to this important subject not just a personal experience of burnout, but a keen eye to the Bible, and wise pastoral insight into the pressures many of us face in ministry.

From the foreword by **ALISTAIR BEGG**

This book is for everyone—not just people in ministry—because we all live very busy lives and are susceptible to burnout. Christopher Ash speaks plainly, wisely and encouragingly. As I read through this book, I found myself evaluating my own life, and found comfort as I recognized my limitations and took to heart his advice.

TIMOTHY S LANE
President of the Institute for Pastoral Care

With clarity, wisdom and honesty Christopher reminds us that we need sleep, rest, time with friends and daily renewal. But God doesn't need any of these things, which is why we can—indeed we must—turn off our laptops, tablets and work phones and leave the study! Our frailty and weakness is part of what makes us human and should drive us to depend on the Lord who made us.

CARRIE SANDOM
Director of Women's Ministry, The Proclamation Trust

In this marvellous and much-needed book, Christopher Ash manages to warn, encourage, expose and comfort in equal measure. Every page is humane, penetrating, rich, wise and above all, gospel-saturated. This book came to me as a word in season from a humble brother, and I am sure God will use it to do the same for many, many others.

GARY MILLAR
Principal, Queensland Theological College, Australia

There are far too many victims of burnout in pastoral ministry. I was very nearly one of them and almost had to pull out after just four years. Christopher Ash's wise counsel, learnt from Scripture and through long, and sometimes bitter, experience, would have helped me enormously in those early years and is still what I need today.

VAUGHAN ROBERTS

Rector of St Ebbe's Church, Oxford and Director of The Proclamation Trust

Reading *Zeal without Burnout* is like sitting across from a godly father and friend who loves you enough to look you in the eyes and say, "the world is not going to come apart at the seams if you take some time off to take care of yourself". Anyone who worships the god of productivity and therefore has forgotten how to take a break will benefit from this book.

NANCY GUTHRIE

Bible teacher and author of the Seeing Jesus in the Old Testament series

Christopher's exposition of the simple truth that "God is God and we are dust" liberates, humbles and strengthens with practical and pastoral wisdom. Read this if you are feeling weary, and be refreshed in God's grace. Read this even if you are feeling energetic because prevention is better than cure!

DENESH DIVYANATHAN

Founding Pastor of The Crossing Church, Singapore

We live moment by moment as frail beings given health and strength by our sovereign Father. May this book help us end the corporate church conspiracy to seem stronger than we are, even omnipotent; and leave us content to keep being wisely weak and daily dependent until Jesus returns.

DR ANDREW NICHOLLS

Medical doctor and church pastor

ZEAL

without

BURNOUT

Seven keys to a lifelong ministry
of sustainable sacrifice

Christopher Ash

Zeal without burnout
Seven keys to a lifelong ministry of sustainable sacrifice
© Christopher Ash/The Good Book Company, 2016. Reprinted 2016 (twice), 2017

Published by
The Good Book Company
Tel (UK): 0333 123 0880
Tel (North America): (1) 866 244 2165
International: +44 (0) 208 942 0880
Email (UK): info@thegoodbook.co.uk
Email (North America): info@thegoodbook.com

Websites
UK & Europe: www.thegoodbook.co.uk
North America: www.thegoodbook.com
Australia: www.thegoodbook.com.au
New Zealand: www.thegoodbook.co.nz

ISBN: 9781784980214 Printed in India

Design by André Parker

ACKNOWLEDGMENTS

My deepest human debt is to my wife Carolyn who walks through all these experiences with me, with consistent patient love and wisdom. He who finds such a wife finds a very great blessing!

I am also grateful to our oldest son John, also in pastoral ministry, whose wise comments (many unacknowledged) pepper and spice up this booklet. And to a number of personal friends, both in Christian pastoral ministry and in 'secular' work, for their wisdom, prayer, and loving support. To Peter Adam and Alain Palacci in particular I am grateful for kind and wise counsel. Also to my former colleagues at the Proclamation Trust (especially my former PA Beckie Hollands) for their wisdom and loyal support.

Alistair Begg graciously invited me to be part of the team at *The Basics* pastors' conference at Parkside Church, Cleveland, Ohio, in May 2014, at which I first gave the seminar on which this material is based. I am grateful to him and to the pastors who engaged with the material and encouraged me.

Above all else, I am thankful to the God and Father of the Lord Jesus, whose covenant love is great and whose faithfulness endures for ever, by whose grace and mercy my name is written in heaven.

Christopher Ash
June 2015

CONTENTS

FOREWORD

by Alistair Begg

Senior Pastor of Parkside Church, Cleveland

As a younger minister, I was invited to give a semi-nar at a conference. I surprised myself by offering to address the matter of "ministerial depression". While I could not speak about this from personal experience, I had sufficient awareness of what it meant to be "bat-tling the blues" to say something about my encounters with post-Sunday listlessness, irrational fears about health, and a realistic sense of insufficiency.

I was taken aback by the size of the crowd that came to the seminar. They were not there for the speaker. I was a "no-name" at a conference filled with "big names". So the reason for the standing-room-only crowd was simply the subject matter. I can still recall how some of the questions asked by lay-leaders displayed an alarming lack of awareness of the nature of pastoral stress. It is fair to say that most congregations are largely unaware of this problem, or do not understand what it means for the pastor and his family to be confronted with burnout. It is no respecter of persons and the challenges are not unique to the 21st century.

Five hundred years ago, Martin Luther knew what it was to be overwhelmed and, although he would have been unfamiliar with the terminology of burnout, his tendency to bouts of melancholy seem to fit the pattern.

Elijah's encounter with the prophets of Baal left him burned out and fearful before the threatenings of Jezebel. He speaks as one who has lost perspective: *I've had enough. take away my life. I might as well be dead.*

Before we critique his reaction, we do well to take stock of those occasions when, after the "success" of ministry, we have found ourselves similarly undone. Returning from a meeting where we were enabled to be of spiritual help to others, we are suddenly and acutely aware of our inability to help ourselves. Through no fault of our own, we may find ourselves isolated and in need of fellowship and encouragement.

If Elijah serves as a warning, Nehemiah provides an encouragement. He understood that there is no "I" in team. The completion of the wall-building project in record time, was in part a testimony to his ability to delegate. He would have burned out faster than a firework were it not for his well-conceived plan to have a division of labor that made perfect sense to all involved, and which was so effective that it met with severe opposition.

Charles Simeon also faced severe opposition in his early ministry at Holy Trinity Church, Cambridge. Apart from the animosity he encountered, the routine challenges of shepherding the congregation were such that his candle was in danger of burning out. His answer was to delegate: he established a "Visiting Society" and appointed a man and a woman church member to be responsible for the pastoral care of homes in their particular district.

Even so, in 1807, after twenty-five years of exhausting ministry, Simeon was close to being burned out. Following a sermon, he would feel "more dead than alive". After a long period of weakness, and believing that he had run his course at the age of 60, he records how, on a visit to Scotland, as he crossed the border, he found himself being, "almost as perceptibly revived in strength as the woman was after she had touched the hem of our Lord's garment". He sensed God redirecting his desire and doubling, trebling, quadrupling his strength; and as a result, Simeon renewed his commitment to his pulpit and preached vigorously for seventeen more years, until two months before his death. As much as I would like to use this story to underscore the benefits of visiting my homeland, we are better served by acknowledging how God so often allows his ministers to come to an end of themselves in order that they might begin to be more useful in his service.

That is why I am delighted to commend this powerful little book. Christopher brings to this important subject not just a personal experience of burnout, but a keen eye to the Bible, and wise pastoral insight into the pressures many of us face in ministry.

I pray that it would help us both to guard against the dangers of burnout and to heed Paul's exhortation to "Never be lacking in zeal but to keep our spiritual fervor, serving the Lord." (Romans 12 v 11) Or as Eugene Peterson paraphrases it:

> *Don't burn out; keep yourselves fueled and aflame.*

STORIES FROM THE EDGE

He stared vacantly out of the window. So much to do. So little energy. His open Bible glowered, chiding his failure to read, work, wrestle, write. His in-box and in tray ticked up and up, each task whispering, "So much to do. So many people. Such deep needs. So little time. So little energy." Prayer burdens stacked up, day after day after day.

After these years of effort and pressure, he had nothing left. No resources, no emotional reserves, no intellectual energy, nothing. And so he stared with empty eyes.

How had it come to this? Could he have done things differently? Might it have been avoided? Is there even now a way out?

Burnout is a terrible price to pay for Christian zeal. Sometimes it cannot be avoided. For some, their circumstances mean there is no other way to live sacrificially for Jesus.

But sometimes it can. For many of us there is a different path. One that combines passionate zeal for Jesus with plodding faithfully on year after year. I want to write about this path. This is a very personal book; and I trust it is a biblical book. But it is very far from being a comprehensive or expert treatment of the subject.

I write for all zealous followers of Jesus. Perhaps especially for pastors and Christian leaders ~ to those entrusted with pastoral oversight under God. Some of us have the privilege of being set free from other jobs to devote ourselves to this work; others combine pastoral leadership with "normal" secular work.

But I write also for the many keen Christian men and women who, in addition to "normal" life ~ busy jobs, parenthood, and so on ~ labour sacrificially to serve in their local churches. The young father holding down a pressured job but also teaching the church youth group. The unmarried woman bearing the weight of much responsibility in her workplace, but also heavily involved in pastoral support and care in her church. The older couple whose gifts and skills are in great demand both at work and in church. And many others like them.

I have a personal interest in the subject. At least twice I have come to the edge of burnout. By the grace of God I have been enabled to step back from the brink.

The first time was in the early days of leading a small church plant in the east of England. I had come from a larger church with a big staff team, but now I was the only paid member of staff, trying to lead a church of a hundred or so adults, with a fair number of children. After a few months the pressure got to me, and I too found myself staring vacantly out of the window, drained and struggling to keep going. With a supportive church council and a month or so of reduced responsibilities, I recovered.

Another time was much more serious. I had been working for eight busy years leading a Bible training course in central London. In September 2012 I returned from an intense ministry visit to Australia and Singapore to begin an eagerly anticipated sabbatical term. I was looking forward to some weeks of refreshment, holiday, fruitful study, and some writing. My wife, Carolyn, was looking forward to sharing those weeks with me. Instead, I hit the wall. When the adrenalin stopped, I crashed. My energy plummeted;

my mood dipped sharply; my morale went through the floor. And I felt empty, used up, expended.

Although I did return to work in January, I was far from firing on all cylinders; my kind colleagues picked up the extra workload for the next six months, and it was not until September, a full year later, that I had partially recovered my energy and morale. It was a painful and sobering experience. I still feel the scars.

I am not alone. In the USA it is estimated that some 1500 people leave pastoral ministry *each month* due to burnout, conflict or moral failure. The causes are diverse, but they show the intense pressure that many in Christian ministry find themselves under. A third of pastors say they feel burned out within just five years of starting ministry, and almost a half of pastors *and their wives* say they have experienced depression or burnout to the extent that they needed to take a leave of absence from ministry. [1]

And it is not just those in formal pastoral ministry. Many zealous Christians juggle the responsibilities of pressurized work and busy family lives, with a desire to serve the Lord in the church as Elders, Bible-study leaders, or ministry with children and young people. Those of us who are pastors can be guilty of underes-

---

1 statistics quoted from *Today's Pastors* (2014) by George Barna.

timating the stresses they face as they seek to serve the Lord in ways that are often invisible to us.

~

One of the pastors and scholars whom I most admire, and from whom I have learned much, is Peter Adam. Peter was senior minister in a large city-centre church in Melbourne, Australia. As a young unmarried man he worked long hours and loved his work. Until, quite without warning, one Monday morning he awoke and began spontaneously to cry, and found himself unable to stop weeping.

His breakdown was very serious indeed. By God's grace he continued in ministry and went on to became principal of a theological college (Ridley College, Melbourne), and the author of a number of scholarly and widely valued books. Nevertheless Peter has continued to live and serve Christ in the shadow of that breakdown. He says he has never since then been able to work more than 50 hours in a week. Through this long experience of frailty, Peter says he has learned to trust God more, and also realised that God can use our weaknesses as well as our strengths.

Peter is senior to me. But let me give another example, from someone much younger.

After working at a church in London while training, my friend is now serving in cross-cultural mission with his wife and young children. He pastors a church plant in Japan. He is one of the most zealous and focused Christian workers I know.

He came back to the UK recently on home assignment (furlough) and just ~ only just, with much help and support ~ recovered enough to make it safe for him to return to his work overseas. Here is what he wrote to me:

> *My own personal experience was that leading a church plant, having a young family and particularly the pressures of preaching every week [in Japanese] led to a reservoir of accumulated tiredness and unrelieved stress which led to various symptoms, including digestive problems, increased irritability, reduced ability to focus on prayer and sermon preparation, failure to keep commitments, mild depression, etc. Nothing to force me to stop what I was doing or even claim sick leave, but enough to make me ask questions as to whether it was sustainable ... later on having a debrief with a medic with professional experience in this area, there was a clear case to make that I was well on the road to likely (humanly speaking) irreversible emotional and physi-*

cal breakdown. In God's mercy we got rest at just the right time.

I wonder what you make of those stories, and the others that you will encounter throughout this book. I imagine some reading this will find them hard to relate to.

You know about zeal, energy, joy in ministry, loving the work of Christ, working all hours and revelling in it. You know about Christian ambition, seeking to achieve great things for Christ. But when someone talks about breakdowns, burnout, hitting the wall, then ~ if you are honest ~ you find yourself thinking that these are things that people ~ middle-aged people! ~ talk about when they have lost their first love for Jesus.

But there will be others reading these words now who know exactly what I am talking about, whether in your own painful experience or in the stories of pastors, Christian workers, or other keen Christians dear to you. And it is worth remembering that none of us thinks we are on the path to burnout until we are nearly burnt out; it is precisely those of us who are sure we are safe, who are most in danger. We need to heed Paul's warning:

So, if you think you are standing firm, be careful that you don't fall! 1 CORINTHIANS 10 v 12

I want to share with you in this book a perspective that God has burned into me as I have both experienced burnout in myself, and met with and supported others who have struggled with the same issues as I have. They have, for the most part, been fine, radiant Christians whose zeal for the Lord and his work has led them to overwork and then collapse.

As someone who has spent the last decade training young men and women for Christian service, I have been keen to help them see that the best kinds of ministry are, more often than not, long term and low key. I have tried to prepare them for a marathon, not a short, energetic sprint. In other words, to help them have a lifetime of sustainable sacrifice, rather than an energetic but brief ministry that quickly fades in exhaustion.

I want to focus our minds on a neglected truth from the Bible about ourselves as people, and our loving God; and to consider seven ideas or principles that flow from it.

I want to warn those of us who think this will never happen to us, and encourage those of us who know only too well that it can and has. I have included the stories of men and women who have experienced burnout, but who have subsequently found comfort, help and a new way of sustainable service.

It is my prayer that this book will help many of my brothers and sisters to maintain their zeal without knowing the bitterness of burnout.

Sacrifice
is not the same as
Burnout

B ut first, let's begin with an objection: *why not burn out for Jesus?* After all, did not the Lord Jesus say something to that effect?

> *"If anyone would come after me, let him deny himself and take up his cross daily and follow me. For whoever would save his life will lose it, but whoever loses his life for my sake will save it."*
>
> Luke 9 v 23-24 (ESV)

Surely the right response to this challenge from the Lord is to throw ourselves wholeheartedly into his service and the service of his gospel, and not to set limits to our self-giving. So why not burn out? What is wrong with burning ourselves out for Jesus? "I would rather wear out than rust out" as George Whitefield said. Is it not selfish and unspiritual to guard myself against burnout?

The problem is that we do not sacrifice alone. It may sound heroic, even romantic, to burn out for Jesus. The reality is that others are implicated in our crashes. A spouse, children, ministry colleagues, prayer partners and faithful friends, all are drawn in to supporting us and propping us up when we collapse.

My colleagues at work rallied around generously to help me; but it cost them in time and energy ~ resources they could otherwise have poured into gospel work elsewhere. Peter Adam has spoken movingly of the friends God gave him to support and pray for and with him; no doubt it cost them too.

There is a difference between godly sacrifice and needless burnout. When I first gave an earlier version of this material at a pastors' conference, I suggested a partial parallel between burnout and self-harm. I did so cautiously, for self-harm is a terrible thing. What I mean is this, that burnout and self-harm share this character, that each damages strength and life to no good effect.

After the seminar, a fellow pastor wrote to me. He said this:

> *It's been very helpful to me to contemplate the difference between burnout and sacrificial living for the Lord. Your reflections ... really helped me to understand the difference. I put it into terms of fighting fire as I'm a volunteer firefighter as well as being a pastor. Obviously you have to push yourself physically when fighting a fire. It's a stretching experience that is uncomfortable and physically difficult. You have to know your limitations while making the sacrifices needed to get the tasks done that must be done.*
>
> *It's foolishness to ignore your limitations, try to be the hero, and cramp up, pass out, or have a heart attack while in a burning structure because you're beyond the limits of what God has supplied you with the capability of doing. It's a form of heroic suicide that is counterproductive because you're now no longer effective in fighting fire and the resources that were dedicated to fighting the fire are now dedicated to saving you.*

I like the analogy with firefighting. The aim is not to be a lone hero, but to work with other firefighters to stop the fire. In a similar way, the aim of gospel work is not to be a lone hero, but to work with other gospel workers to spread the gospel of Jesus.

My reason for writing this book is to help us discern the difference between sacrifice and foolish heroism, and so to guard against needless burnout. We are to be *living sacrifices* until God takes us home to be with Jesus, we are to offer ourselves as those who have a life to offer, rather than a burned-out wreck.

Paul calls on us to be living sacrifices:

> *Therefore, I urge you, brothers and sisters, in view of God's mercy, to offer your bodies as a living sacrifice, holy and pleasing to God ~ this is your true and proper worship*   ROMANS 12 v 1

A "living sacrifice" is a strange expression. It means a sacrifice that goes on and on being offered, so long as life lasts. When I am off work because of exhaustion, my body has little to offer; I may feel in pain but the sacrifice is barely alive. How much better to keep plodding on in Christian service if we can.

Perhaps the expression "sustainable sacrifice" gets to the heart of the idea ~ the sort of self-giving living that God enables us to go on giving day after day.

~

Before we get into the meat of this study, I want to say clearly and forcefully that we are *called to sacrifice,* and sometimes that sacrifice will damage or even destroy us in this life.

A substantial part of my own experiences of near-burnout was caused by factors outside of my control ~ the loneliness of Christian mission as a teacher in a school with little fellowship; later, the pressures of inadequate staffing in the church I pastored; then a training team I led; the costly privilege of caring for elderly parents, and so on.

Sacrifice is costly, and our brothers and sisters in the persecuted church will have much more radical stories to tell. It will be a great mistake if you get to the end of this little book and resolve to have an easy life!

But let us explore together what sustainable sacrifice might look like, and how to avoid ~ or recover from ~ unnecessary burnout.

Here is how we are going to come at the question. I want to begin with a very big neglected truth, and then draw out four simple and very practical implications of that truth, before concluding with three radical questions about our motivation.

ROY'S STORY

Monday July 2nd 2012 is burned on my memory. I climbed on board a crowded Tube train that morning to go to my office. But I was not looking forward to work. I had a difficult meeting with a colleague first thing that morning, and I had been worried about it all weekend. I picked up a free paper and started to read, but as the train got closer to my destination, I felt a crushing, agonising weight on my chest. *"I'm having a heart attack,"* I thought, and staggered to the door at the next station.

I collapsed on the platform bewildered, with my hand on my chest. I gasped *"Somebody help!"* and then lost consciousness.

I spent the next 24 hours at the hospital, where the surprising verdict was that there was absolutely nothing wrong with my heart. I had suffered an extreme panic attack. But when I returned home, not only could I not face work, I simply could not face people ~ I didn't want to have anything to do with anybody. I shut down from life completely.

Colleagues who were not aware of what was wrong joked that I had timed my illness to perfection so I could watch the Olympics. Nothing could be further from the truth. I sat in a chair day after day with the TV switched on. But I was oblivious to anything that was happening on the screen in front of me. Nothing registered.

~

How had I arrived at this point?

What I suffered that morning, and what followed, had been building for a long time.

I had been in ministry for over 20 years. The last ten years I had spent working for a large evangelistic organisation. I was utterly passionate about reaching people for Christ, but I had joined an organisation that was in the throes of a massive reorganisation ~ much of which involved painful "downsizing".

The morning I was made a Director, I went to visit the Christian workers at one of our centres. They were congratulating me on my appointment; but I had come with bad news; their project was closing, and they would likely all lose their jobs.

Christian organisations place a very high value on relationships. We expect more from one other. We care deeply for each other. I am naturally a people person. Outwardly extrovert, but I feel things very strongly. So as we wrestled with the organisational changes as a leadership team, there was a lot of emotional pain and heart searching involved. I don't think any of us realised how high the personal cost was to us.

I was carrying a lot of heartache from seeing fine Christian people having to move on, and the organisation was carrying a lot of relational damage. Everything we did as a leadership team was questioned by the staff. And differences of opinion emerged about our personal and organisational values as we tried to rebuild the organisation.

My default position was that *"If I look after the people, the organisation will look after itself"*. The main leader viewed things the other way round ~ *"If we create a good organisation, then the people will work well and be happy"*. We all cared about the people, but what might seem like a subtle difference actually led to a lot of worry and misunderstanding. In public we were united, but management meetings were very stressful for all of us. Unbeknown to me, the main leader was also going through a breakdown.

~

I was off work for three months. At the time, I never thought about my experience as being burnout. But I went through a period thinking *"I will never get back to work"*. I know that it is not like this for others, but on 16th September it was like a light switch went on, and

I suddenly thought *"I can go back to work now"*.

The organisation had been fantastic. Very caring, and utterly discrete about what was going on with me. The HR director told me that it takes as long to settle back into work as the time you have had off. This was wise advice, and proved correct. I approached work cautiously for the first three months, but then another light-switch moment, and I said to myself: *"You're OK now"*.

In faith terms, I never felt that God was distant. But it troubled me deeply that I was unable to read ~ even the Bible. I don't even remember praying much at all ~ I just felt incredibly secure, and that God was with me.

This is where my evangelical heritage came to the rescue. Although I couldn't read, the Bible was not lost to me. As a young Christian, I had memorised Scripture avidly. I had always found this useful in evangelism, and the pastoral care of others ~ being able to quote relevant scriptures to others. But now it came home to me in a new way. The word was hidden in my heart, feeding me, and assuring me at my lowest point. By memorising God's word, I had invested in my own soul and it was now paying dividends. God took me by surprise by how alive the word is in my heart. When I resumed work, I had to force myself to read the scriptures again as part of the discipline of my faith.

I realise too that part of my issue was a lack of real love. When things were difficult at work, it is easy to criticise the management, but the greater work was something that needed to happen in me. We are an evangelistic organisation. Proclamation runs through our veins. But we also need to love one another. Jesus said that this was the way people would know that we are his disciples. By not loving my colleagues, I was compromising my values, and the work of the organisation.

Surprisingly, I now feel that my capacity for work has actually increased ~ because I now work differently, more effectively. I take more active time for reflection on my work and priorities. Take more time to apply the Bible to my work, even when that cuts across the thing I am trying to achieve. There's always more we can do in ministry, but God is not asking "Can you do more?". He is asking "Do you love me?" Some of those extras are not always as vital as we think them to be.

A neglected
TRUTH

We are
creatures of dust

Sustainable sacrifice is shaped by wisdom and rests on self-knowledge. The foundation of all I have to say is that *you and I are dust*. We need to know that and never to forget it. You and I are embodied creatures; we are dust.

God made us out of dust:

> ...*the Lord God formed the man of dust from the ground...* GENESIS 2 v 7 (ESV)

And one day he will turn us back into dust:

> *You turn people back to dust, saying, "Return to dust, you mortals."* PSALM 90 v 3

God is God and we are dust.

Oh, yes, it is wonderfully true that by God's grace Christian believers are indwelt by the Spirit of the One who raised Jesus from the dead. And yet:

> *...the body is dead because of sin*
>
> ROMANS 8 v 10 (ESV)

That is to say, our spirits are alive by the righteousness of Christ and the indwelling of the Spirit of Christ, and so at the resurrection our mortal bodies will be given resurrection life (Romans 8 v 9-11). But in this age our bodies are "dead"; that is to say, they are mortal, decaying, coming from dust and returning to dust.

We must not allow ourselves to slip into a false spirituality that treats our bodily existence as if it can be separated from our so-called "spiritual" life ~ as if our spiritual life carries on quite independently from what is happening to our bodies.

This is an old heresy. In one of its earlier phases it was called Gnosticism; but it has a way of popping up in new disguises. No, we must remember that we are whole people: embodied people whose existence is "of a piece" and whose bodily and mental lives are inseparable from the way we relate to God (our "spiritual" life).

Dust is disintegrated matter. It is the polar opposite of complex interconnected cells, organic systems, neural pathways, nerves, muscles, bones, tissues, the whole wonderfully woven system that is a living human being, "knitted together" in the womb by the power and wisdom of God (Psalm 139 v 13).

A living human being can walk, run, build, think, speak, act, love. But dust is disconnected particles on the ground, with no life, no action, no agency, no power; it is lifeless, inorganic matter. You and I came from dust and our bodies will return to dust. At no point of our lives in this age are we far away from reverting to dust. We are very fragile.

The trouble with being strong and healthy is that you and I begin to believe we are something other than dust into which God has temporarily breathed the breath of life. Because I can walk, think, talk, and act, I begin to believe I am immortal ~ that I will always be able to walk, think, talk, and act. But I won't.

In Western countries, we live in an age of unparalleled wealth and health. Not for all, it is true, but for many. In both the USA and the UK, male life expectancy has increased by roughly a decade over the period 1960-2010.

Worldwide, men are four inches taller on average than a century ago. And so we begin to feel that health and strength is normal. It isn't.

It is very sobering to see a human being return to dust. My father died in 2014, aged 95. He landed with the first wave of allied troops on D-Day and was awarded the Military Cross for conspicuous bravery in the weeks of hard fighting in Normandy that followed. All his life he was a strong man. Until three months before his death he was walking, talking, even driving a car. And then, quite suddenly, some falls reduced him to a shadow of his former self.

In the space of a few weeks he faded away; he could not walk, his thinking became confused, and finally he died. My dad was a believer, so his death is sweetened with Christian hope. But it is still sobering and grievous to watch a strong man return to dust.

And yet it is a healthy thing for you and me to see, and to remember that this is what will happen to us. Whether suddenly or gradually, whether in youth or old age, God will say, "Return to dust, child of Adam". He may say that today or in twenty years' time; but the moment God says that, we will return to dust. How strange to think so proudly about ourselves and our strength when we are so fragile.

One of the memories I will never forget from my year of nervous exhaustion is the forceful reminder of my fragility and mortality ~ of body and of mind. Your health and strength, like mine, is a temporary thing. It will not last long. God can take it away at any time, in a small measure or in large measure, suddenly or gradually.

Some of us are well aware of this in our bodies as we pass through middle age and parts of us stop working so well (or at all). We know they will never work again the way they did in our teens or twenties. But it is also true of our minds.

O the mind, mind has mountains; cliffs of fall
Frightful, sheer, no-man-fathomed. Hold them cheap
May who ne'er hung there...

So wrote that strange troubled poet Gerard Manley Hopkins. And he is right. There are mountains ~ sheer cliffs in the human mind.

I remember as I crashed into breakdown the terrifying feeling that my mind was becoming unhinged, that I was balanced precariously over a precipice, that beneath me there were dungeons of despair and sloughs of despond from which I might never escape. That is a frightening thing. Some who read this will know even more of that same terror. Later, I will suggest where help may be found for those struggling with such fears.

But for the moment, I want to say that it is a healthy thing, a realistic truth, to grasp that I am dust. I am made from dust. In this mortal life I will never be more than a few particles of dust into which God has temporarily breathed the breath of life. I am frail and fragile, and I do well never to forget it.

You and I are all different. We differ in stamina, both physical robustness and mental strength. We have differing abilities to sustain longer or shorter hours of work. Some of us travel well, others less well. We have different capacities in many ways. But whatever our God-given constitution, each of us is no more than dust.

When God "signed" you and me for his team ~ if I may use the analogy reverently ~ he knew he was not signing another god. That is what managers in the NFL, the English soccer Premier League or the Major League think and hope they are doing. They pay vast sums of money in the transfer market because they hope the linebacker, the striker or the pitcher they are signing will prove to be a sporting god (or at least a demigod).

It is not so with us. When you and I surrendered to Jesus as Lord, we did not offer him the services of a divine, or even semi-divine creature to strengthen his kingdom; we offer him the fragile, temporary, mortal, frail life that he has first given to us. That is all we have to offer. God knows that.

For he knows our frame; he remembers that we are dust.
PSALM 103 V 14

God is under no illusions about who he is getting on his team.

There are, I want to suggest, seven keys to sustainable sacrifice. And we turn first to four implications of this foundational truth of our mortality and our dependency upon God. Four ways in which God keeps us alive in this age, four needs we have that God does not share.

We need sleep, *but God does not.*
We need Sabbaths, *but God does not.*
We need friends, *but God does not.*
We need food, *but God does not.*

God has, as someone put it to me, "put the medicines on the table and we need to take them". So let us consider each in turn.

BEN'S STORY

I come from a long line of working people. My grandfather a son of the soil. My father a son of toil ~ a strong man who worked gruelling days in construction. My mother equally strong and determined to provide for her family. So I grew up in a home where we were constantly told that we must never be afraid of hard work; that hard work was the way to "get on in life". It was our family tradition, and we took pride in it.

It's a sense that I absorbed into my mindset. I was the first in my family to become a Christian. I was also the first to get a College education. I approached my studies with determination, and the career I subsequently embraced brought its rewards as I sought to be diligent and to go the extra mile.

Every spare moment was given over to serving in church. Leading the work with teenagers; active in evangelism; organising camps and preaching. And when marriage and family came, the pace did not slacken. I was strong. God had gifted me. I was made for service. What else should I do?

I wonder whether all along, I harboured a superior attitude towards others. Pride was crouching at my door. As I saw others in less demanding jobs, with smaller families who seemed to be "coasting" at church, I would secretly think: "they are not pulling their weight".

The letter to the Hebrews warns: *"See to it that no one falls short of the grace of God and that no bitter root grows up to cause trouble and defile many"* (Hebrews 12:15). Despite being a dedicated gospel-hearted Christian who preached grace, the truth is that I was dangerously close to living a gospel of works, not grace.

An older brother in my congregation recognised the signs. He had himself experienced significant burn-out in his time. In conversation one day he said to me: "Ben, you need to humble yourself before God, or he will humble you ~ and it will not be pretty".

Unrecognised by me, there were stresses at both work and home. I was failing as a father and husband. I was feared at work, not loved. I was being a false witness to Christ ~ and I was excusing it all by convincing myself that it was the Lord's work I was doing.

I don't know what wreckage would have ensued if I had not pulled up short, prompted by my pastor's wise counsel. Seething anger was not far beneath the surface, and I suspect that burnout for me would have involved cruel words, arguments, grand gestures and raging self-justifying tantrums, rather than depression.

I was humbled by this realisation.

The pride I felt at being a hard worker, had turned into something that was ugly and ungodly. I needed to repent.

Part of that was owning up to my mistakes with my wife and children, and with work colleagues. Part of that was realising that whenever I said "Yes" to something, it meant saying "No" to something else. Usually my family were the ones to suffer.

I had always "known" that God is sovereign, and that the Lord did not need me to fulfill his kingdom purposes. But that was theoretical knowledge. I now try to practice that truth in my decision making. I am thrilled to have the opportunity to serve. It is a privilege to be invited into God's gospel work in the world. I know that the strength God has given me is something that has its limits and is not mine to take pride in.

I know that I am dust.

Seven
KEYS

1.
WE NEED SLEEP
and God does not

The God who watches over his people…

> *… will not slumber … he will neither slumber nor sleep.*
>
> PSALM 121 V 3,4

He is ever watchful, ever wakeful; he never needs to doze off and never loses his watchfulness for a nano-second. This is a wonderful assurance.

～

But you and I *do* need sleep; it is a fundamental mark of our mortality. If we neglect this, we are implicitly claiming an affinity with God that mortals should never claim.

God never needs to sleep and never sleeps. But the psalmist rebukes us when we behave as if we don't need sleep:

> *In vain you rise early and stay up late, toiling for food to eat ~ for he grants sleep to those he loves.*
>
> PSALM 127 V 2

The context in Psalm 127 is that it is the LORD, the covenant-making God of the Bible, who "builds the house" and "watches over the city" (Psalm 127 v 1); in the context of the Psalms of Ascent (Psalms 120 ~ 134), the most natural understanding of the "house" is the Temple, and the "city" is Jerusalem.

So the project that God watches over is not your or my private-life projects, but the great project of building the people of God, ultimately the New Jerusalem under "great David's greater Son". In this age, that project is Christian gospel work; everything that serves the gospel of the Lord Jesus. It is in this context that we hear the rebuke to sleeplessness that comes from "anxious toil".

The Bible does not rebuke us when we work hard for Jesus, for such hard work is consistently commended in the Scriptures; notice, for example, the refrain of those commended for their hard work in Romans 16. Priscilla and Aquila are Paul's fellow-workers (v 3); Mary "worked very hard" for the church (v 6); Urbanus was another fellow-worker (v 9); Tryphena and Tryphosa "work hard in the Lord" and Paul's dear friend Persis is "another woman who has worked very hard in the Lord" (v 12).

Hard work for Jesus and his church is a good thing.

Nor does the Bible rebuke those who make sacrifices for Jesus and his gospel. Paul himself had sleepless nights (2 Corinthians 6 v 5; 11 v 27) necessitated by mission. His friends Priscilla and Aquila "risked their lives" for him; Andronicus and Junia were in prison with him (Romans 16 v 4, 7). This too is a good thing.

No, the rebuke of Psalm 127 is to those whose sleeplessness is caused by "anxious toil": burning the candle at both ends because *we will not trust God for the work*.

Sleep seen through this lens is an expression of trust in God. You and I sleep because we do not believe that the project of building the people of God rests upon us; we sleep because we know that God never slumbers or sleeps.

Even the incarnate Word ~ the Word made flesh ~ needed to sleep. He was tired: so tired that he slept on a cushion in a fishing boat in a raging storm (Mark 4 v

38). To be human means to need sleep. We need sleep to restore energy. Sleep is the daily way our Father gives us to do this. We neglect it at our peril.

How strange it is for us to be proud of our energy and ability. One day we feel we can conquer the world. One sleepless night later we are reduced to gibbering, incoherent wrecks! It is what one of my sons calls a "pinprick grace", a reminder of our fragility.

Sleep is a strange and puzzling phenomenon. We know what it is to have deep and restful sleep and to wake refreshed. We know what it is to have too little sleep. We know what it is to have plenty of hours in bed and yet to wake not feeling refreshed. We know something of peaceful sleep and troubled sleep. But we do not really understand what makes the difference between them. Good sleep is a gracious gift of God.

But what we must not do is to burn the candle anxiously at both ends of the night because we will not trust God for our work and Christian service. I think to myself: "I can get another hour's work done just now, or early tomorrow morning, just to squeeze in a little extra and do that bit more in serving Jesus".

For sure, there are times when an early-morning start may be just what is needed; but let's not think we can follow that with a late night of working and another early start, so that late nights and early starts become endemic to our pattern of work. That would be a manifestation of a refusal to trust, and a cocky imagining that we are somehow just a little bit superhuman, a cut above our ministry colleagues. Like the manna in the wilderness, rest is an exercise in trust.

UNSOCIAL HOURS

One of the problems for those engaged in Christian pastoral ministry is that pastoring often involves unsocial hours. Whether we are "full-time" pastors or not, we need to be with people when people are free to be with us. That may mean evenings and weekends. So it is not easy to be fully in control of our sleep patterns.

But we need to be careful.

We need to look at the regular shape of our week and make sure there is enough time for sleep. God may or may not give us good sleep ~ that is his sovereign choice ~ but if we don't allow *time* for sleep, he can't possibly give us the restorative slumber we so need!

It is worth considering how best to wind down later in the evenings, perhaps avoiding stimulants before bed, keeping away from flickering screens, caffeine or things that stimulate the mind and heart too much. Just as a runner winds down after a race, so we need to wind down after the day, to commit people and troubles that are on our minds to the One who does not sleep, and then to go to rest.

If you are married, make sure you leave pastoral struggles and burdens outside the bedroom door. Deliberately, intentionally, share together and pray together before heading for bed. The husband who says, as they are dropping off to sleep, "Oh, I forgot to tell you about my conversation with…" can with one sentence ruin his wife's sleep; and *vice versa*! Either tell one another earlier and pray about it together, or hold it until the morning.

～

Here are some ideas for ending a day well:

- *Give yourself a quiet few minutes to look back on the day* and to pray for the people whose burdens you share, either on your own or with your wife or husband. Do this before getting ready for bed.
- *Then do something that will help you wind down.* Perhaps an episode of some not-too-emotionally-demand-

ing television series, or a quiet chapter of a book unrelated to your work or Christian service. Something that will slow your body and mind towards sleep.

- *Keep a pad of paper by the bedside,* so that when urgent or important things pop into your head, you can make a note to deal with them the next day ~ and then forget about them for the night.
- *End the day by looking back at a Bible verse with which you began the day,* as a reminder of a truth about God. I use a notebook by my bedside to jot down a thought, usually from one verse in my morning Bible-reading; even if I have managed to forget it during the day, it is then easy to remind myself what it was!

CARRIE'S STORY

I hadn't been sleeping well for some time but car-
ried on working, thinking that a more normal sleep
pattern would emerge eventually. I was working with
students in a large city-centre church and regularly
worked 14-hour days during term time.

I just *loved* the work I was doing and didn't think the
long hours were a particular burden ~ just part of the
intensity of student ministry. I always took a day off
each week and usually spent it seeing friends who lived
elsewhere ~ leaving early in the morning and driving
back late at night to maximise the time.

After about six months I went to see my family doctor
and was shocked when she signed me off work for a
month saying I was exhibiting the symptoms of major
stress and needed to stop. I hadn't told any of my colleagues anything so it was rather a shock to them too.

But it wasn't until I did stop that I realised how bad
things were ~ and for a while they got *much* worse (something my doctor said would happen). The sleepless nights
were caused by an addiction to adrenalin that was beginning to have a negative effect in other ways ~ I wasn't
eating properly, had an overly high metabolic rate, a lousy
digestive system and suffered from heart palpitations and

cluster headaches. My concentration levels nose-dived, I couldn't read anything, found decision-making impossible and started withdrawing from people.

I thought a month off was all I would need to get back to normal but I was completely wrong. At the end of that first month the doctor signed me off for another month and then another. After three months I went back to work part-time but within a fortnight was signed off again.

During my first visit, my doctor said she had seen this kind of illness before and reckoned I wouldn't fully recover unless I let the job go ~ so there was absolutely no pressure on me to get back to work. I told her I really didn't think that would be necessary ~ but after three months off and no obvious progress in my recovery, I began to realise that she was right. After another month off, I again went back to work part-time but the same thing happened.

Two months after that I resigned…

Carrie's story concludes on page 100

2.
WE NEED
SABBATH RESTS
and God does not

We need sleep; God does not. Second, we need Sabbath rests, and God does not. God the Father is always working (John 5 v 17); 24/7/365 he sustains the universe, upholding and ruling with his sovereign providence.

The "rest" of God in Genesis 2 does not mean he takes a break from governing the universe; it is the rest of having completed the creation he has made. But God works tirelessly to sustain creation, to feed creation and to govern creation by his providence. He does not sleep and he does not take Sabbath rests. *But we must.* If we neglect this, we are implicitly claiming an affinity with God that mortals cannot claim.

Readers will no doubt have different understandings of the significance of the Sabbath commandment for Christians today (Exodus 20 v 8-11), and I have no wish here to enter into those debates. But I hope we can all agree that the "six day ~ one day" pattern of work and rest is hard-wired into creation and therefore into the human race. Behind the Sabbath commandment lies a creation pattern. Even if the Sabbath is no longer an old-covenant religious obligation, we are simply foolish to behave as though we no longer need a day off each week.

~

Some years ago a senior doctor wrote:

> *We doctors in the treatment of nervous diseases, are compelled to provide periods of rest. Some of these periods are, I think, only Sundays in arrears.*
>
> SIR JAMES C. BROWN, THE TIMES, 30TH APRIL 1991

Even those of us who are generally careful to keep a weekly day off find it very easy to let the discipline slip.

Suppose, for example, that Saturday is your regular day off; on all the other six days you are busy with draining work or costly Christian service. And then you are invited to help with some church meeting on a Saturday. It seems so worthwhile. You are keen to do it. Before you know it, you've said "yes". And then you look at the diary and find there is something immovable on every other day that week. So there is no possibility of taking a full and proper day off in that particular week. "Ah", you say to yourself, "never mind, it's only one week".

In some ways the worst thing that can happen is that you get away with it. God in his mercy gives you strength for that extra commitment; you get through the following week with plenty of energy. And you begin to think ~ subconsciously perhaps ~ that somehow you have evolved into some slightly superhuman creature; your fellow Christians need their weekly days off, poor ordinary mortals that they are, but you, no, you find you can manage without...

Or can you?

And so, all too easily, it becomes a habit. You sit more and more light to your day off, until it becomes a rarity, or a single snatched evening, afternoon or morning. It becomes something that happens in a good week, but rarely in a normal week.

A young Christian worker was off work with exhaustion recently. I asked him about his days off. He replied that "most weeks I only have off half a day" and admitted that this might sometimes be due to "bad time management". That honest confession reminds us that one key to a successful day off is six hard-working days on!

We live in an age of endemic distraction, in which concentration is perhaps more difficult than ever. The internet can be a horrendous time-waster, as well as a useful tool. We need to make sure that when we work, we work; this will make it much easier to stop when we stop.

Of course, serving Jesus is about loving people. And, as we know, people are complicated and unpredictable. They (and we) do not fit into tidily-planned diaries. They have crises. Bereavements are not planned in the diary; nor are sicknesses, breakdowns, accidents, relational flare-ups and family catastrophes. So there should be a right raggedness about a keen Christian's diary, and especially the pastor's diary.

But it is important also to say that love does not mean always jumping when somebody calls. There are crises; but there are also many pastoral needs that can perfectly well wait until after your day off.

There are events for which we rightly drop everything, cutting into a day off, or curtailing a holiday. I remember a dear brother ringing to tell me his father had taken his own life; of course I dropped everything to go round immediately to weep with him and pray with him and his wife. I would have come back early from holiday for that. I know that many reading this would make that sacrifice to walk through the valley of the shadow of death with those we love.

But for every desperate trauma there are perhaps fifty or more pastoral needs which can perfectly well wait for a later visit or meeting. Indeed, it is often good to wait, so that our brothers and sisters learn to depend upon God rather than upon a particular Christian. A wise measure of self-preservation and the drawing of boundaries around our time is not the denial of love, but the outworking of wisdom.

God needs no day off. But I am not God, and I do.

This is very humbling, especially for the keen Christian who feels the need to sort everybody out. Our problem so often is that we want to punch above our weight. The great Scottish minister William Still puts it like this:

> *Some meddling ministers want to sort everybody out. God is not so optimistic. There are some who will die mixed-up personalities, and they may be true believers … Don't try to do the impossible. Know your*

> *limitations, and know what God is seeking to do in the world and what part in it He wants you to play … Most people crack up because they try to do what God never intended them to do. They destroy themselves by sinful ambition, just as much as the drunkard and drug addict. Ambition drives them on."*
>
> FROM THE WORK OF THE PASTOR

My wife Carolyn and I have a little informal liturgy we use when one of us is burdened by some distressing pastoral need and longs to be able to sort it out and solve the problem for the person concerned. A crisis of faith, an entanglement with the world, a troubled marriage, a dysfunctional family, a distress, inveiglement into some idolatry ~ whatever it is, we long to be able to set the person back on the track of strong faith and consistent godliness.

And yet we can't.

So Carolyn says to me, or I say to her:

> *Remember, there is only one Saviour of the world; and it's not you, and it's not me.*

Peter Adam wrote to me to say he had recently spent an hour and a half with a young Christian worker and said to him repeatedly, "God has already appointed his

Messiah, and he did not appoint you."

This humbling assurance and conviction is key to maintaining the necessary discipline of a weekly day off. It is an outworking of the acknowledgment that I am dust and God is God.

3.

WE NEED FRIENDS
and God does not

The third implication I want to explore is friendship. God has no need of friendship. Within the eternal fellowship of love that is the "Three in One" God, there is a perfection, a beauty, and a sufficiency of friendship (and more) that needs no addition from outside. God has no need of us. His love overflows and draws us into fellowship with himself; but it is a love that is uncaused; he has no need of our friendship. We are not to picture God as lonely and unfulfilled without us.

But while God has no need of friendship *outside* the fellowship of the Trinity, *we do.*

God has so created us that we are social beings and need one another for healthy life on earth.

When God says that it is not good for human beings to be alone (Genesis 2 v 18), he is not saying that sex is the answer to human loneliness, for it is not; he is saying that through the creation of the first woman, he enabled the first man and woman to begin the procreation of the human race, in which human fellowship and friendship is a necessary and good part of the created order. Whether married or unmarried, we are created to be together with others.

$\sim$

One of the most encouraging examples of friendship in the Bible is that of Saul's son Jonathan with David. On one occasion when David was in great trouble, we read that Jonathan went to meet him "and helped him to find strength in God" (1 Samuel 23 v 16). Friends that do that for us are very precious.

If we neglect friendship, we are implicitly claiming an affinity with God that mortals cannot claim.

Vaughan Roberts has helped many of us to see the importance of friendship, especially for men in our culture, who "do" friendship less well than many of our sisters in Christ. His book *True Friendship* is so helpful. We need to develop and sustain healthy Christian friendships. A younger Christian worker said to me that his near-breakdown was partly caused by lack of sustaining friendships. We who are keen to serve Christ need to watch over one another in love.

One of the best things I did during my year of nervous exhaustion was to restart a prayer triplet with two other men. I should have done this years before, but somehow it had been postponed until the crisis came.

We began to meet most weeks. We were honest with one another about our struggles, our perplexities, and our joys; we tried to stir one another up to fight the good fight of faith and persevere in love and good works; and we prayed for one another, both when we met and in between times.

~

Some years ago, a well-known preacher was leading a church in the city where I was an assistant minister. I had never met him. But I remember someone commenting to me that no one really knew who was close to him ~ who his friends were. It ought to have set alarm bells ringing for us. But somehow he was so famous and his preaching so fruitful that we didn't worry.

And then, quite suddenly, he left his wife in a shocking and public scandal, and was lost to Christian ministry. The absence of close friendships, with all the healthy accountability that goes with them, ought to have been a warning sign for him, as it should be for us. Let us take care to nurture and sustain such friendships, and all the more so when we serve in contexts where there is much mobility and endless change of people. We are dust. We are not created to be autonomous, go-it-alone, god-like pastors.

If, like me, you are not a natural at building and sustaining friendships, I want to encourage you to persevere and to be intentional about it. Some of us in a world of social media have a great many Facebook friends but very few, if any, deep friendships. It is good to be deliberate and make the hard calls as to which are the friendships into which we will invest the limited time we have.

One problem I have is that I imagine my friends will feel it is a bit of an imposition if I ring them up or go and see them ~ that in their heart of hearts they are happier with rather more distant friendships. Perhaps I am not alone in this, and I think it says more about me than about them! But I suspect many of us ~ especially men ~ need to try a bit harder at being good friends.

One particular problem can be for pastors moving to a new area and new church. How can we develop good friendships without seeming to have favourites? How is it possible to have the kind of openness about our own feelings and struggles with members of our own congregation?

Opinions differ about the wisdom of making our closest friends within the churches we serve. Personally I have not found this a problem, but that is because my closer friends had the maturity not to exploit their friendship with the minister to increase their power or influence within the church. But whether we develop friendships within our own church fellowship or outside it, we must surely work at making strong friendships.

A WORD FOR MARRIED COUPLES:

Sustain Intimacy

This is an appropriate point for a word about sustaining intimacy in marriage.

In 1 Corinthians 7 v 1-6, Paul engages with wrong teaching in Corinth. Some were saying that "It is good for a man not to have sexual relations with a woman" (verse 1) ~ probably meaning sex within marriage, rather than discouraging people from getting married in the first place. "It would be more spiritual," such people were suggesting, "for a married couple to have sex as little as possible, perhaps even not at all."

The apostle could not disagree more strongly! On the contrary, he says, husband and wife each *belong to one another entirely*, so far as this beautiful intimacy is concerned. On the day they marry, they promise to give to the other all that each of them is as a sexual man or woman (verses 3-4).

Paul reluctantly agrees that they may have a sexual "fast", but only if both *really* agree to this (rather than one *pretending* to agree); and only if it is for a limited period, "that you may devote yourselves to prayer" (verse 5).

The word "devote" is a strong word meaning "to give time and energy to". But notice this: if a temporary pause in sexual intimacy allows a couple to give time and energy to prayer that they would not otherwise be able to give, then it must follow that the maintenance of a healthy sexual intimacy in normal married life also needs the investment of time and energy. For otherwise the temporary cessation would not free up time and energy!

This ought to be blindingly obvious, and yet many of us married couples neglect it. We slip into assuming that healthy sexual intimacy will just happen anyway. It won't, or not in the longer term.

Before I got married, I was (metaphorically) sitting in my red sports car at the red traffic light. I knew that not having sex before marriage was difficult (although I knew it was right), but it never occurred to me that *keeping sex going* within marriage might ever be difficult.

So there I was, just waiting for the light to go green on our wedding day, after which I imagined us driving off into the sunset, enjoying endless delightful times together, without the need for any intentionality on our part. Surely it would *just happen.*

I may not be the only bridegroom to have entertained such unspoken thoughts.

The truth is, as any couple knows once they have been married for more than three weeks, it doesn't *just happen.* A healthy intimacy needs deliberate cultivation by both partners. Intentionality, time and energy.

There are plenty of factors outside of our control that may make this difficult, including physical and psychiatric illnesses, work pressures, unavoidable times apart, childbirth, the exhausting demands and lack of privacy that come from a busy family life, and then ~ in due course ~ the whole process of ageing.

There may also be particular pressures in pastoral leadership that make things difficult, including unsocial hours of work and emotionally demanding and burdensome pastoral engagements with people.

But not everything is outside of our control. There are things about our lifestyles that we *can* control. It is our responsibility under God to do all we can, each to satisfy and love the other in this lovely way. Do not let this beautiful relationship shrivel up and die for lack of nurture. Sometimes the poor state of married intimacy is a telltale sign that all is not well with our lifestyles; it may be an early warning sign on the road to burnout.

4.
WE NEED
INWARD RENEWAL
and God does not

So, as creatures of dust, we need sleep, Sabbaths, and friendship. God needs none of these.

The final need I want to focus on for us as human beings is inward renewal. Just as we need food and water to keep our bodies physically alive, so we need the inward renewal of the Holy Spirit in our hearts and lives.

What I mean is this: as a creature born from above, a man or woman in Christ, I am no longer merely dust; I am dust in whom the Spirit of Christ lives.

Although the outward me is disintegrating, heading downwards inexorably towards returning to dust, ageing, weakening, losing my power and faculties ~

there is within me the Spirit of the One who raised Jesus from the dead (Romans 8 v 10-11). He is the down-payment of resurrection life. And so, in parallel with the outward decay, there is an inward renewal day by day (2 Corinthians 4 v 16).

The point I want to make is this: we are *embodied beings*, and the renewal of the Holy Spirit is not a "spiritual" process, if by "spiritual" we mean something separate from what is happening in our bodies and minds. Although it is helpful to think about the different components that we are made of as human beings ~ our bodies, minds, emotions, etc. ~ this should not blind us to the reality that God has made us as whole, integrated creatures.

Our physical nature, our mental life, our emotional, intellectual and affectional facets of life are inseparable from the "spiritual" part of us. So spiritual renewal is not something that operates just on a hidden part of our being ~ it actually affects the way we feel and are in this life. It brings us things like joy and peace ~ and even physical bodily refreshment in the reality of life.

This is why I think it is a mistake to consider renewal by the Holy Spirit as separate from renewal in our embodied well-being, our bodies, our emotions, our affections and our thoughts. Times of quiet, enjoyment of beauty, the experience of refreshing exercise, stimulating sport, wonderful music, wholesome reading and conversation, can at their best be God's handmaidens to spiritual refreshment, as they are combined with hearing afresh the promises of God in the gospel.

One of the ways in which we are made in the image of the Creator is in our creativity. This will express itself variously: for some it will be speaking, for others writing, for one the making of music, for another through art. But however God has made us creative, let us seek to ensure there are outlets for that creativity. Stifled creativity has a deathly, dulling effect on our souls. Freedom to be creative stirs up the wells of creativity in our hearts, that we may thrive in the image of a wonderful Creator.

"Come with me by yourselves to a quiet place," says the Lord Jesus to his disciples, "and get some rest." (Mark 6 v 31). It is not that a quiet and beautiful place brings us closer to God, for it does not, but rather, that things like this can refresh our spirits.

You and I are all different in our personalities. One of many helpful things my kind and skilled Christian doctor said to me during my year of nervous exhaustion was this:

Think about the kinds of things that drain you and the sorts of things that energize you. Try, so far as it lies within your power, to put in the diary sufficient of the things that energize you to keep your emotional, physical, intellectual, relational batteries topped up.

I suppose it ought to have been rather obvious, but I needed to hear it. Since then I have tried to be intentional about this.

The kinds of experiences and activities that drain or energize us will differ from personality to personality. I remember standing talking to a friend at a party. As we looked around at the cheerful hubbub of conversation, he said to me, "Some people are energized by this. But I am drained." So was I. We escaped from the gathering as soon as we decently could! But others will have stayed as long as they could.

Some will be more introvert, as I am, refreshed by quiet reading, study, reflection and only certain kinds of conversation. Others will be energized by people, almost indiscriminately. I am glad for them, but I will shrivel up and become a pathetic, sleepless stressball if I have too much of that.

It is the same with physical and mental activity. For some, attending a sports match will be refreshing;

others will hunger for a quiet art gallery. Some will revel in a slow, quiet walk in the woods; for others a run or a vigorous bike ride does the trick.

It is good to develop a healthy self-knowledge about what energizes us ~ what the Holy Spirit uses to bring us that inward renewal. But these activities will never be enough on their own to bring us true spiritual renewal.

Each of us needs our personal devotional times with God: times of Bible reading and prayer, times to be glad to be in Christ, times of thoughtful reflection before the Lord: times to be refreshed. It is not selfish to guard those times, any more than it is selfish for a firefighter to take a break before heading back into the fire. Indeed, if we do not give space for renewal, there will soon be nothing left of us to give.

BEWARE MINISTRY MACHISMO

Until recently, I lived in the centre of London, where, as in many vibrant cities, there is a somewhat cocky workplace machismo. "I'm working harder than you," is the culture, "and therefore I am more important than you. Indeed, it is necessary for me to let you know how hard I work, for only then will you truly appreciate how important I must be."

It is not surprising that we can detect this culture seeping from the world into the church. We get kudos from how hard we are seen to be working.

Please pray for me. It's been very, very busy for the past few years. I do have to work long hours, travel a lot, get rather little sleep, and often have to sacrifice my day off.

That is what I say with my lips, but the subtext in my heart may be this:

I want you to realize that I and my ministry are very important ~ and probably more important than you and your ministry.

Such ministry machismo is proud and dangerous. To neglect sleep, Sabbaths, friendships and inward renewal is not heroism but *hubris*. It is to claim that I am a level or two above normal members of the human race. When a fellow-Christian lets slip how very hard they are working, and that they haven't had a proper day off for a while, we need to find a way of saying to them (in love!), "You are behaving like an arrogant fool!"

What is more, they will not just harm themselves. A friend in ministry wrote to me that one of the hardest things in his near-breakdown was "feeling like I was being *expected* to work at least as hard as I was, rather than being encouraged to be realistic and take a rest".

I am so grateful that when I was an assistant minister, I was under a wise leader who understood this so well. He had a remarkable ability to work very hard. He guarded his days off and was very disciplined, and he certainly could work harder than me.

But he never put pressure on me to work as hard as he did.

When I needed a break, he actively encouraged me to take as much break as I needed. I knew he thought none the worse of me for that. I thank God for that godly example and oversight. Those of us in leadership should try to emulate his example with the expectations we lay ~ or do not lay ~ on others.

ALISON'S STORY

I magine being given your dream job. That's how I felt when offered the opportunity to create a new range of Bible-reading notes for children. I threw myself into the task with great excitement.

I had been employed for several years at a church as a youth and children's worker, then in a busy schools' work team. Evenings and weekends were taken up with church work. I was no stranger to hard work, and it was no bother to me.

But thrilled as I was about writing Bible notes for children, I have a *particular* passion for helping families explore the Bible together ~ so I wanted to write a complementary set of notes for families at the same time ~ and in one stroke doubled the size of the job!

What followed was five years of hard, hard work. For those outside, writing for a job might seem fun, creative and relaxing. But the reality is that writing for children seems almost tailor-made to suck the energy out of you! It needs to be clear; funny; exciting; and, crucially, biblically-faithful writing ~ all of which raised the pressure on me considerably.

It sapped my intellectual, creative and physical energy ~

day after day after day. It was exhausting, and took longer than we'd expected, which meant it became completely normal to work long hours every day, and most Saturdays and Public Holidays as well.

And this is where ministry passion became a problem. In many jobs, someone could have said: "This is ridiculous, you need to ease up". "But this is ministry", I said to myself. "This is gospel work." And we had children and families waiting for each new issue. So I kept on going.

It may sound as if I was working myself into the ground ~ but it didn't feel like it. Yes, I was tired, but I was also just as thrilled by the opportunity given me as I'd always been.

And I thought I was getting away with it unscathed. I've always been pretty healthy ~ hadn't seen a doctor for ten years ~ hadn't taken a day off work in fifteen (and was proud of it!). I always had masses of stamina. I was genuinely someone who could burn the candle at both ends and in the middle as well.

Which is why it was such a shock when I got ill.

~

I knew how hard I was working, and how tired I had become. But it genuinely never occurred to me that I might get ill. That happened to other people. Not me.

Some Christian friends insisted on taking me to a doctor. I was convinced I was fine, but the doctor diagnosed depression. I simply didn't believe her. I didn't feel depressed, or seem to have any of the "classic" symptoms. It took months to be convinced, but it turned out she was right.

That was over ten years ago, and the Black Dog of depression has been my constant companion. Sometimes overwhelming, at other times distant, but a brooding presence that I'm told will always be with me.

Was my illness simply the result of five years of overwork? Probably not.

Did the burnout contribute to me becoming ill? Probably.

Could the depression have been prevented? Hard to say, but it seems likely that it was waiting for me like a ticking bomb.

Could the exhaustion and burnout have been prevented? Yes ~ but I can understand why it wasn't. It's hard to get someone to slow down when they are passionate about their ministry. And, as a single person, there was no one at home to see the late nights and the toll they were taking.

When someone seems to be working all the time, they're often accused of being a workaholic. I wonder if a Christian version of that might be a "zealaholic"? It's not that we want to work just for work's sake ~ but maybe that we allow our passion for ministry to overtake other issues and, as a result, we find it easy to make unwise choices.

I still have these tendencies, but with supportive friends, church and work colleagues, I have found a working pattern that is sustainable for me. And I've learned that it's still ok to push myself hard at times, so long as I build in time to rest and re-energise as well.

Vitally, I've learned that God is truly sovereign in all things. This illness has taught me that God is not dependent on me ~ he doesn't need my "achievements" to work out his good purposes. It's me who is dependent on him and his goodness.

5.
A WARNING:
beware celebrity!

For several years I taught through John's Gospel with my students. Every time I worked through the material, I found my heart searched by the teaching in John 5. The Jewish opponents of Jesus accuse him of "making himself equal with God" (verse 18), in the sense of setting himself up as a rival of God. No, says the Lord Jesus, I do only what my Father does; I seek his glory and not my own. He says to his critics:

"I do not accept glory from human beings".

VERSE 41

But they do, and this prevents them from believing:

> *"How can you believe, since you accept glory from one*
> *another but do not seek the glory that comes from the*
> *only God?"* VERSE 44

The trouble is that by nature I seek and value the glory that comes from the praise of other people. What other people think of me matters far too much. I fear I am not alone.

Many of you reading this will be predisposed to burnout. You are capable; you have many natural abilities. If you are in pastoral ministry, you might have hoped for a successful career in the secular workplace. Perhaps you came into pastoral leadership after such a successful career, or in the early days of what might have become a secular success story.

You were used to, or might have expected to enjoy, the praise, respect, high regard, and the applause of people in the world. But now you have chosen a work the world despises, or at best considers marginal and odd. You and I may easily seek substitute adoration from our own flock, or from our fellow-pastors, to fill the gap left by the absence of affirmation from the world. And we may become proud loners, seeking self-fulfilment through our work.

Or perhaps you are still in that successful career, but

serving wholeheartedly in your local church. The prestige and status given you by that career matter to you more than perhaps you realize. The wholehearted local-church service you squeeze into a busy life gives you very little affirmation and praise from others. It is tempting to pitch our energies into the activities that result in praise from others.

I am ashamed to say that I am like that by nature. I want you to say how helpful you have found my ministry. I want you to blog that this book has been helpful to you! I would love you to wave it in front of your congregation and say it is the best thing you have ever read on the subject. That is what I want, by nature. But I suspect I may be speaking to a fellow glory-hunter.

You too want the people in the church you serve to think well of you. If you are a pastor, you want your fellow pastors to admire you. When asked at a pastors' conference how things are going in your church, you want to be able to reply like this: "Well," you say quietly, "when we planted the church there were three old ladies and a three-legged dog; now there are 30,000 young, gifted, lively men and women, 3,000 doing an enquirers' course, 300 people on the church staff, and a budget of $30 million. And we only planted the church three weeks ago."

"Isn't God good?" you add modestly!

But the Lord Jesus says that seeking the praise of people *prevents* real faith in our hearts.

Beware celebrity! We live in a secular culture of celebrity; it is all too easy to let that culture of people praising people infect our churches and conferences. Beware putting speakers and pastors on pedestals. Beware heroes. "Do not put your trust in princes" (Psalm 146 v 3). Beware wanting to be on such a pedestal yourself. Search your heart.

Pray that, by some wonderful supernatural ministry of the Holy Spirit, in your heart and mine there will truly begin to be a desire that God be glorified. Pray that Jesus will grow greater and we will grow less (John 3 v 30). And pray that we will care less what people think of us and more what they think of Jesus.

I ask myself how much of my overwork over the past decade was driven by an honest desire for the glory of God? And how much by a desire that people should think well of me and my ministry? I trust there was some of the former; and some of the overwork was the result of inadequate staffing, as is so often the case in Christian work.

But I wish I knew the full and honest answer, for my heart is deceitful and desperately corrupt (Jeremiah 17 v 9). And I cannot plead innocent, and I doubt if you can either.

This rebuke to our self-centred motivation is a sword into the depths of our twisted, dark hearts. We follow a Master who "did not please himself" (Romans 15 v 3, one of the great understatements of Scripture). If we buy into the church culture of celebrity, we drift away from following Jesus faithfully.

∼

That is the warning. Now for the encouragement ∼ and we certainly need it!

DENNIS'S STORY

I was preaching one Wednesday night when, in the middle of the sermon, I packed up my notes and walked off the stage ~ with no explanation to the congregation. I had just had it, and I wasn't going to take it any more.

I drove home thinking, "I'm not going back. I'm finished with ministry. In fact, I may even be finished with church."

By the time I got home I couldn't stop crying. I shut myself in our bedroom and didn't leave the room for three days. My wife came in and prayed, but I knew I was done with ministry.

~

Burnout can be defined in many ways, but that's how it looked in my situation. The seeds of this meltdown had been planted years earlier, and I had unknowingly nurtured them, carefully tending the soil and watering the plant until finally it sprouted into a very ugly weed. I was oblivious to what I had been doing and never would have guessed I could end up in such a state.

During seminary, I pastored a small church just outside of Kansas City for three and a half years. It grew from some thirty-five souls to almost three hundred. I liked the feeling of "success". After seminary, one growing church led to the next until I was called to a mega-church in another state.

Once I settled in, however, I discovered the church was rife with problems. I uncovered dishonest staff members, strife between members, and a legacy of incomplete truths being offered to the church. Members no longer trusted the staff. I had never encountered such serious problems before.

Furthermore, my predecessor was well known in the community because of the church's television broadcasts. He was a flamboyant personality who preached powerful evangelistic sermons. His departure was sudden and unexpected, and most of the church grieved the loss. By contrast, I was in my mid-30s and more of a Bible teacher than evangelist.

To my shock, a number of people didn't like the new guy and left. Attendance reports and contribution spreadsheets confirmed my unpopularity. People wrote to me, telling me that I was ruining the church. Some even turned away when I approached them.

What did I do to turn things around? Did I pour my

heart out to the Lord? Did I accept being rejected if it meant obeying him? Did I trust the simple preaching and teaching of the word? Nope! I tried every trick in the book and worked longer and harder.

The sad truth is that the gimmicks worked ~ but I felt ashamed and guilty.

Then a church in Tennessee contacted me. It was bigger ~ and nicer ~ and they really wanted me. I jumped at the chance for a new beginning and success in another city and didn't look back. The overused cliché, "The definition of insanity is trying the same thing over and over and expecting a different result" described me to a T. I attacked my ministry with the same work hours, drive and methods.

But at this church I inherited a new set of problems. People were loyal to my predecessor, who had remained in the church. They were unwilling to change and certainly didn't mind telling me so. I pushed harder for my agenda. As I worked harder and harder in my own strength, the pressure built higher and higher until that fateful night when, like an overheated radiator, the boiling hot water blew off the cap and spewed out. The car could go no more. I was used up and burned out.

~

Is there hope for recovery from burnout? Absolutely! The Lord used a number of people and events to change my life and approach to ministry. My wife listened to me, challenged my faulty thinking, and spoke reality to me. Most of all, she prayed for me.

Deacons and staff members came to our house, and insisted on talking with me. Their expressions of grace were life giving. As I slowly recovered from the burnout incident here's what the Lord taught me:

- *Focus on the Lord's definition of success.* Ministry isn't about numbers. It's about faithfully preaching, teaching, and loving the people.
- *Seek help from a mature Christian friend* or Christian counselor when appropriate.
- *Share the load* ~ with staff, elders, deacons, and trusted friends and members.
- *Don't neglect your spiritual, physical and mental health.*

A year after my burnout incident, the Lord called us to the church where I've spent the last twenty-three years. It was a much smaller church, but the people loved the Lord and his word. And they've loved and cared for me throughout the years.

The church has tripled in size, but I've refused to

focus on numbers or gimmicks. I've not allowed myself to slip back to old ways of thinking and motivations, and God has faithfully healed old wounds.

Recovery happens when we come back to being spiritual men and women who do spiritual things God's way.

6.
AN ENCOURAGEMENT:
it's worth it!

Discouragement is deeply demotivating. You and I sweat away in preparation and in one-to-one Christian encouragement with somebody, we labour in prayer, in church leadership or service, and there seems so little fruit.

An individual you invested in falls right back into sin. A church you lead splits or is stagnant. You preach your heart out and someone smiles and tells you they enjoyed the humorous aside you included in the middle; and your heart sinks. The youth group you help with is going badly. If you have been in ministry for any length of time, you will know all too deeply what I am talking about. I asked one youth leader how his group was going; he grimaced and said, "Disaster!" ~ and then told me the story, which amply supported his assessment.

Discouragement is that little voice on your shoulder, whispering in your ear that all your hopes and aspirations are nothing more than youthful naïvety. There is no point persevering.

How corrosive that little voice is; how ruinous to gospel zeal and drive!

~

I love that exchange in John 4 where the disciples come to Jesus at the well in Samaria and urge their weary Master to eat something! And Jesus replies,

> *"I have food to eat that you do not know about... My food is to do the will of him who sent me and to accomplish (finish) his work"*   JOHN 4 V 31-34, ESV

This is what gets me out of bed in the morning, says the Lord Jesus. *I have been sent; I will do the will of the One who sent me, and finish the work he has sent me to do.*

To walk in the footsteps of Jesus is not a recipe for pastoral idleness. For the finishing of that work took Jesus to the cross, where he cried at the last, "It is finished!" (John 19 v 30, using the same word translated "accomplish" in John 4 v 34, ESV). But it is a very deep encouragement. Jesus' work ended ~ so it seemed ~ in failure. He was betrayed by a close friend. His other followers deserted him. Almost nobody believed in him. He failed: he was crucified in weakness. And yet "he will see of the fruit of the travail of his soul and be satisfied" (Isaiah 53 v 11, RSV).

And we too may know that nothing we do in Christ, for his glory, for his gospel, will ultimately be in vain. For the bible says to us…

> *Always give yourselves fully to the work of the Lord, because you know that your labor in the Lord is not in vain.* 1 CORINTHIANS 15 v 58

I love to read and re-read Psalm 90. It is so full of our frail mortality and God's eternity. And yet it ends with the prayer,

> *Establish the work of our hands for us … yes, establish the work of our hands."* PSALM 90 v 17

So we are authorised to pray like this:

Lord, make my life of service worth something;
make it sure.

  May it be that, at the end of time, this collection
of dust, this temporary mortal frail feeble sinful
Christian may have achieved something by your grace
that will last to eternity.

God gives us this prayer to pray. In an Ecclesiastes world of frustration under the sun, in which stuff just goes wrong, people mess up, in Jesus Christ there is such a thing as lasting fruit. I may not see it, but I know it is there, and so I can say, "It is worth it".

And yet you and I cannot *plan* this fruit, and we cannot *measure* it. We cannot even *strategize* for it. It is the gift of God.

I don't know about you, but I love to plan, and I love to be in control. I am somewhere on the OCD spectrum; I live by lists, schedules, plans. There is no harm in that, so long as we at least half expect our plans to be thrown out of the window. As a friend wrote to me:

  The gospel teaches us that in the world, in ourselves,
and especially in the realm of word ministry, sin has
caused catastrophic disordering. And yet so often we
make plans without contingency or room for leeway ~

as if the most likely thing is for everything to go as we plan and expect.

But it won't. I had set aside some study and writing weeks for a particular writing project about two years ago. I was powering along happily, keeping to time. And then sickness intervened: my elderly father was taken ill and eventually died, my dear mother needed much care, and all writing has stopped, and all I could do was urgent administration and preparation. That project will have to wait until some future date before I can resume it. *That ought not to surprise me.*

Gospel ministry is ministry in a messed-up world. And there is grace in the disruption, for it humbles me; it shows me afresh my total dependence upon God.

So you and I cannot plan for fruit; neither can we measure it. The stuff we can measure is the unimportant stuff: church budgets, church buildings, pastors' reputations, numbers, numbers, numbers ~ even professions of faith.

But the really important stuff ~ changed hearts ~ cannot be measured. God in his grace sometimes gives us a glimpse, an encouragement, some evidences of grace. But it can't be measured. You pray for someone and they don't change. Who knows but they may change years later under someone else's ministry (*I planted, but Apollos watered*). Or the fruit may come after you die. I don't know; you don't know. But we *do know* that in the Lord Jesus our labour is not in vain.

CARRIE'S STORY

Concluded from page 56

It took me the best part of a year to recover fully and I couldn't have done that without the practical, financial and prayerful support of family and friends, but I know letting go of the job was the turning point.

One very dear friend asked me what I missed most about student ministry and I said without hesitation, "the one-to-one Bible studies". These were the bedrock of all the discipling I was involved in.

It had been pretty scary when I realised I couldn't concentrate on reading the Bible with others anymore and I wondered if I would ever do any ministry again. My friend said to me:

*"Carrie ~ the Lord won't love you any less if you
never do any one to ones again, and he won't love you
any more if you do!"*

How helpful it was to hear those words and, in the ten
years or so since then, I have often recalled them ~
and passed them on to others!

Looking back now, I think the signs of burnout had
been there for a while ~ but I hadn't noticed them or
if I had, I chose to ignore them. I'm much more aware
of them now and have taken steps to ensure that the
workload I take on is more sustainable.

I'm generally much better at planning my diary and
saying "no" to things, and feel more aware of my limitations, which only increase as I get older. I'm also
much better at accepting that it's okay to do what I can
in the time that I have, and so I no longer try to prepare things "perfectly" by burning the midnight oil ~
not that I ever managed to prepare anything perfectly
when I did.

The key things that will help us avoid burnout are
knowing ourselves and the season of ministry we're in,
letting others know us so we don't become isolated,
choosing our role models carefully, remembering to
stop and smell the roses, knowing how to relieve stress

(in a non-addictive way), and recognising that we all have different work capacities.

But perhaps the most important thing I have discovered is this ~ the Lord doesn't need us to do his work and it isn't what defines us. I was as much a child of God ~ chosen, holy and dearly loved ~ when I was ill and unable to work as I am today.

Some of us have had to learn that the hard way.

7.

A DELIGHT:

rejoice in grace, not gifts

Finally, a delight. Here is an exhortation that has meant much to me recently. I have been reading through Luke's Gospel in my personal devotions with J.C. Ryle's *Expository Thoughts*. Some weeks ago I was reading the mission of the seventy disciples in Luke 10. And how the disciples:

> *returned with joy, saying, "Lord, even the demons are subject to us in your name!"*

And how Jesus exhorts them:

> *"do not rejoice that the spirits submit to you, but rejoice that your names are written in heaven."*

> LUKE 10 v 17-20

Joy is a great motivator. What touches and warms the heart? What gives joy? I remember when I was very gloomy about my pastoral work some years ago, and a friend (now in glory) asked me, "Do you enjoy it?" "No!" I replied, "I certainly don't". But even as I said it, I knew it was dangerous. You and I *ought to* enjoy ourselves, in the deepest sense.

But how? There are two alternatives: we may enjoy gifts or we may enjoy grace. We may enjoy whatever is the equivalent for us of the demons submitting to us in Jesus' name; or we may enjoy that our names are written in heaven.

If joy is to motivate us to gospel work, then joy must be rooted in something outside of the fruits of our work, something that can't be touched by the vagaries and frustrations of this life under the sun.

Ryle is so perceptive about this. Of course we want ministry success, he says.

> *Success is what all faithful labourers in the gospel field desire … All long to see Satan's kingdom pulled down, and souls converted to God … The desire is right and good. Let it … never be forgotten that the time of success is a time of danger to the Christian's soul. The very hearts that are depressed when all things*

> *seem against them, are often unduly exalted in the day*
> *of prosperity. Few men are like Samson, and can kill*
> *a lion without telling others of it (Judges 14 v 6) ...*
> *Most of Christ's laborers probably have as much suc-*
> *cess as their souls can bear."*

When our joy comes from our gifts and our success, we will *always* be under pressure. For we are only as good as the last sermon, the last youth talk, the last spiritual conversation, the last few months of Christian service, the last success.

It is bad for us, but it also has dark implications for others. Because if we adopt this mindset, we will contribute to a culture of works in which all zealous Christians feel the pressure to succeed, the expectation to keep working harder and harder; a reluctance to take the breaks we need.

Trimming a few hours off my sleep, cutting into a few days off, cutting time for friendships, depriving my wife of intimacy, neglecting personal refreshment ~ if these "sacrifices" can push my ministry just a step or two above my peers, then I shall be truly joyful.

This is the voice of the enemy. And it always leads to disillusion in the end.

What is the remedy?

~

The remedy is to glory much in grace.

It is a privilege to be used in ministry; but it is a much greater privilege to be *recipients* of grace. We value gifts so much ~ gifts in speaking, preaching, persuasion, apologetics and leadership. Those who have them are proud of them; those who do not have them admire them too much.

But, says Ryle,

> *Men forget that gifts without grace save no one's soul, and are the characteristic of Satan himself. Grace, on the contrary, is an everlasting inheritance, and, lowly and despised as its possessor may be, will land him safe in glory.*

So let us strive to keep grace as the main thing.

Ryle concludes, in vintage fashion:

> *Without such marks (that is, of grace) a man may have abundance of gifts and turn out nothing better than a follower of Judas Iscariot, the false apostle, and go at last to hell. With such marks, a man may be like Lazarus, poor and despised upon earth, and have no gifts at all.*

But his name is written in heaven, and Christ shall own him as one of his people at the last day.

CONCLUSION
I will serve the Lord

The main emphasis of this book has been avoiding needless burnout. I have assumed that those reading this are, by grace, filled with zeal and generally hard working. Here are some concluding thoughts for us to consider.

A. DON'T BE SOFT!

In other circumstances and for different readers, it might be necessary to emphasize not being so frightened of burnout that we take no risks and fail to throw ourselves wholeheartedly into the work of Christ. We may need reminding of the challenge of the Lord Jesus:

> *"If anyone would come after me, let him deny himself and take up his cross daily and follow me. For whoever would save his life will lose is, but whoever loses his life for my sake will save it"* LUKE 9 v 23,24

B. DON'T DESPAIR!

Some reading this will be close to despair. You recognize in your own life many ~ if not all ~ of the symptoms of incipient burnout. And you wonder if there is a way back.

I want to encourage you always to leave room for the grace of God in your life. And to take resolute action and seek help. Don't be afraid to seek skilled and wise medical help. Talk urgently to those to whom you are accountable; and if you are not accountable to anyone, seek appropriate accountability as a matter of first importance.

Be prepared to be *very firm* in changing your lifestyle and patterns of Christian service, even if it is hard.

The better you are at your job, the more pressure will be put on you just to keep your head down and press on. Sometimes it is only those very close to us who can see the toll we are paying; for me, I am so grateful to God for my loving and observant wife, Carolyn, who saw more clearly than I did that urgent change was needed.

A pastor in the US wrote to me to say that he has come to realize that his pattern of work was not sustainable in the long term. But his elders were not willing to take seriously the need to do things differently. And so, with sadness, he decided that the only way out was to move to another pastorate. I applaud his courage and salute his wisdom. Would that more of us were prepared to take such firm action.

But when I delivered this material at a pastors' conference in the US, another fellow pastor confided in me that if he were as open about his frailty as I had been about mine, his board of elders would certainly dismiss him.

I cannot tell you how much I was saddened by this. If you are laboring as a Christian in that kind of "works-rather-than-grace" atmosphere, probably you would be better out of it; that kind of board of elders does not deserve to have a pastor at all.

The term "burnout" may cover many different underlying issues in your life. We ~ especially perhaps we who are men ~ must not be too proud to seek help. If appropriate, that will include both pastoral counsel and professional medical help.

But be encouraged that God, in his infinite mercy and patience, always has a way forward that is filled with grace, and that will often include a measure of healing. There may be scars, and some of those scars may be unavoidable; but always there is grace in our weakness.

C. DO A SELF-CHECK

I want to encourage you, whatever your stage of life, whatever your circumstances, whatever your Christian service, to pause and spend some time giving yourself a thorough self-check. Here are some questions that I ask of myself.

- *Am I giving myself enough time for sleep?* Am I developing healthy patterns of "winding down" towards sleep?
- *Am I taking care with regular days off?*

- *Am I investing in godly friendships?*
- *Am I self-aware about how God gives me inward renewal,* and taking care to use his means of grace for that renewal?

And what about my motivation?

- *How much do I care what people think of me as a Christian?*
- *... and do I believe the promises of God,* that faithful service of Christ will bear fruit in the end?
- *Am I rejoicing in the free grace of God towards me* rather than in any gifts I may have?

D. MAKE A RESOLUTION

I hope this short reflection, prompted by my own painful experience, will prove a blessing to zealous Christians, and especially to those in pastoral ministry. I want to encourage you to say to yourself,

> *"If I never preach another sermon, never lead another church meeting, never give another talk, never have*

> *another one-to-one spiritual conversation with anyone,*
> *never use my gifts ever again in ministry, my name is*
> *still written in heaven. And in that I will rejoice."*

That is a far, far greater and more wonderful thing than my Christian service, even if that ministry were to be multiplied a hundredfold. God has reached down to me in Christ, forgiven my sins, cleansed my dirty heart, shone his light into my darkness, given me his Holy Spirit to indwell me and bring me into fellowship with the Father and the Son. What a joy to be his!

With this firmly in mind, we can say to ourselves:

> *"I am ~ and will never, this side of the resurrection,*
> *be more than ~ a creature of dust. I will rest content*
> *in my creaturely weakness; I will use the means God*
> *has given me to keep going in this life while I can;*
> *I will allow myself time to sleep; I will trust him*
> *enough to take a day off each week; I will invest in*
> *friendships and not be a proud loner; I will take with*
> *gladness the inward refreshment he offers me. I will*
> *serve the Lord Jesus with a glad and restful zeal,*
> *with all the energy that he works within me; but not*
> *with anxious toil, selfish ambition, the desire for the*

praise of people, and all the other ugly motivations that will destroy my soul. So help me God."

WHAT EXACTLY
IS BURNOUT?

Dr Steve Midgley

Burnout isn't a medical diagnosis. Come to that nor is "mental breakdown". But our culture sensibly uses both terms because they are good ways of capturing what's involved when someone finds themselves "tipping over the edge".

So what exactly is going on when someone arrives at the point of "burnout"?

Experiments on stress demonstrate the way our performance improves in line with the motivational demand upon us. With little or no motivational drive (either from without or within), there is little reason to perform, so we don't. But as the pressure on us rises, so does our performance. That, for example is why athletes regularly produce performances in an Olympic finals which they would never manage in training.

But that relationship has a limit. At some point ~ the tipping point ~ increasing pressure begins to produce poorer performances. In athletic terms, a commentator might explain a poor performance by saying "it looks as if the pressure got to them". They are describing an athlete feeling so much pressure to perform that they fail to achieve even their normal standard, never mind reach beyond it.

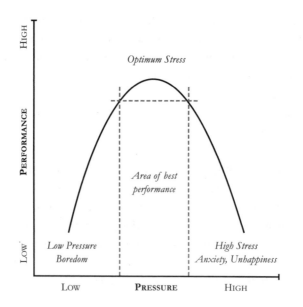

This phenomenon ~ the stress response curve ~ helps us understand what is happening in burnout.

Pressure in our lives produces results. It motivates and energises us. We respond to pressure with raised levels of "stress hormones": adrenaline and noradrenaline. They stimulate, energise and activate us. But these stress responses are designed for short bursts. They are classic "fight or flight" responses and work best when balanced by periods of rest and recovery when we can "recharge".

But constant levels of stress over a long time-period deplete our reserves. This might happen because of persistently long working hours or the tiring effect of prolonged uncertainty of some sort, or the additional demands that caring for a sick relative presents. We become exhausted and demotivated; we struggle to concentrate and to perform.

Sometimes we notice what is happening and take a break. We recover our energies and all is well. But sometimes we push ourselves so many times, over such a long period of time, that eventually the system simply begins to shut down. We burn out.

The overlap with other experiences such as depression and even chronic fatigue is considerable. What begins with burnout may develop into depression.

Where burnout leads to a loss of role or the experience of "failure", it may produce guilt or shame or low self esteem, which get bound up in the experience of low mood and depression.

In other circumstances burnout is mostly experienced as exhaustion and lethargy, and that too can persist in something that takes the form of chronic fatigue ~ though sometimes chronic fatigue develops in the absence of any obviously excessive stress.

We are also each differently susceptible to burnout. Partly this is related to different constitutional and temperamental factors ~ we are all wired slightly differently. And partly it reflects how we have each learned different ways of managing our stress ~ many notice the way that good habits of rest, exercise and sleep have enabled them to cope better with stress.

To some extent our capacity to manage stress is also shaped by our relationship with the Lord ~ the way we turn to him in our struggles really *does* matter. But working out which elements are at play and to what extent in any one individual is never easy. So it's simply not accurate to say that burnout is a sign of some sort of spiritual weakness.

The person who experiences burnout may, in fact, be someone who is much more spiritually sensitive to the warning signs God has put in their way than the next person who muddles along, spiritually oblivious to the growing ungodliness that stress is creating in their life.

WARNING SIGNS

So how might we recognise the warning signs of burnout?

Sleeplessness is a key sign. It's a common symptom of any form of mental distress, and always worth attending to. Low mood, tears, lethargy and exhaustion are other obvious signs that we are getting close to the edge. So too are persistent feelings of nervousness, sometimes escalating into full-blown panic. Less obvious warning signs would be irritability, moodiness and anger.

Of course these are things all of us experience from time to time, but when they keep recurring or when they persist for weeks on end, they may be alerting us to the fact that what is expected and what we can manage are starting to clash.

Poor judgement and consequent moral lapses are another way burnout can make itself known. A need for "comfort" or the desire to get a quick "buzz" can lead to overeating, excess alcohol use, pornography or even illicit sex.

Under pressure we are capable of making poor decisions and that can damage ourselves and others.

PRACTICAL STEPS

What practical steps should we take if we suspect we might be at risk of burnout?

Actually that question highlights the critical problem ~ noticing that we are at risk in the first place. It's generally true that others often notice things about us long before we notice them ourselves. So it makes sense to give others *permission* to tell us when they notice signs that we are under pressure. We should encourage those close to us to tell us if they have concerns. And then we need to listen.

We can also conduct regular reviews. A summer holiday or a retreat is a good context in which to stand back and take stock of the past year. Inviting others to give input to that sort of review would be wise.

Sometimes we can manage change by ourselves. We

may find that what's needed is a new pattern of prayer or a new way of getting exercise or a new commitment to time with friends. Or a bit of all of those. But sometimes we may feel so much in a fog that it takes someone from outside to help us. That could be a wise friend asking good questions or something more formal with a counsellor. Finding someone who can speak gospel truth into our situation will be a great help; we may need to seek that out in parallel to getting professional secular help or medication. Whoever we recruit, it helps if they are intentional. We need someone who will follow up with us and press us to talk regularly and review progress on changes we have agreed to.

Burnout isn't the worst thing that can happen. In fact, it may sometimes be the very thing God uses to challenge us about the need for spiritual growth and change. But it would still be better to arrive at wiser patterns of discipleship before, rather than after, we burn out.

Dr. Steve Midgley is the Executive Director of Biblical Counselling UK. Steve teaches courses in biblical counselling at Oak Hill College and is the Director of the Certificate Course provided by Biblical Counselling UK in association with CCEF. He is Senior Minister of Christ Church, Cambridge and trained as a psychiatrist before being ordained.

Further Reading

Peter Brain, *Going the Distance: How to Stay Fit for a Lifetime of Ministry* [Matthias Media, 2004]

John Hindley, *Serving without Sinking: How to Serve Christ and keep your Joy* [The Good Book Company, 2013]

Paul Tripp, *Dangerous Calling* [Crossway, 2012]

Marjorie Foyle, *Honourably Wounded: Stress among Christian Workers* [Monarch, 2001]

Vaughan Roberts, *True Friendship* [10Publishing, 2013]

Kent & Barbara Hughes, *Liberating Ministry from the Success Syndrome* [Tyndale House, 1987]

Zack Eswine, *Sensing Jesus: Life and Ministry as a Human Being* [Crossway, 2012]

LIVEDIFFERENT

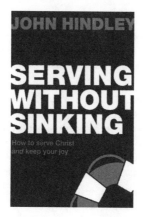

Many of us are serving, and feel like we're sinking. We feel joyless, weary and burdened. John Hindley shows how Jesus was telling the truth when he offered people an "easy yoke"—a way of serving him that is joyful and liberating. He explains why serving is so often joyless—and how our identity in Christ changes everything.

The Live Different series looks at the unseen pressure points Christians face in everyday life. It shows how the gospel provides real answers, freeing Christians to live life to the full.

thegoodbook.co.uk | thegoodbook.com | thegoodbook.com.au

thegoodbook
COMPANY
Opening up the Bible

At The Good Book Company, we are dedicated to helping Christians and local churches grow. We believe that God's growth process always starts with hearing clearly what he has said to us through his timeless word—the Bible.

Ever since we opened our doors in 1991, we have been striving to produce resources that honour God in the way the Bible is used. We have grown to become an international provider of user-friendly resources to the Christian community, with believers of all backgrounds and denominations using our Bible studies, books, evangelistic resources, DVD-based courses and training events.

We want to equip ordinary Christians to live for Christ day by day, and churches to grow in their knowledge of God, their love for one another, and the effectiveness of their outreach.

Call us for a discussion of your needs or visit one of our local websites for more information on the resources and services we provide.

Your friends at The Good Book Company

UK & EUROPE
NORTH AMERICA
AUSTRALIA
NEW ZEALAND

thegoodbook.co.uk
thegoodbook.com
thegoodbook.com.au
thegoodbook.co.nz

0333 123 0880
866 244 2165
(02) 6100 4211
(+64) 3 343 2463

WWW.CHRISTIANITYEXPLORED.ORG
Our partner site is a great place for those exploring the Christian faith, with a clear explanation of the good news, powerful testimonies and answers to difficult questions.